TITLE PAGE

WHEN AUTHORITY IS ACTIVATED
The Atmosphere Shifts

By
TAVACA DORSEY

Published by Vizual Essence Publishing LLC
United States • 2025

EPIGRAPH

**"When the enemy comes in like a flood,
The Spirit of the LORD will lift up a standard against
them."**
— Isaiah 59:19 (NKJV)

COPYRIGHT PAGE

DEDICATION

To God —
the Author of my destiny,
the Keeper of my soul,
the One who awakened what was always inside me,
and the only power who deserves the glory for my activation.

To my daughter —
my legacy, my motivation, and a divine reminder
that generational cycles can be broken
and new spiritual authority can be birthed through obedience.

To my family —
thank you for being a part of my becoming.
Your presence in my life is not accidental,
and your chapter in my story is honored.

And to every reader —
especially those who felt different, silenced, unseen, targeted,
or spiritually "marked" before they understood why —
may this book become the language you never had,
the confirmation you never received,
and the ignition you were born for.

May your activation be recognized, not feared.
May your authority be embraced, not hidden.
And may your journey be Spirit-led, not people-managed.

TABLE OF CONTENTS

CHAPTER 1 — WHEN HEAVEN CHOSE THE DAY

*"He trains my hands for war,
and my fingers for battle."*
— Psalm 144:1

Some days look ordinary from the outside
but are already marked in Heaven
as irreversible turning points.

Activation rarely arrives through
church stages,
public ceremonies,
or prophetic announcements.

It often arrives
at the most unexpected time
in the most unexpected place
with the most silent introduction.

For me, activation did not come
because I sought spiritual rank,
requested deeper sight,
or asked to be called for warfare.

It came because Heaven decided
it was time.

I didn't feel chosen.
I didn't feel powerful.
I didn't feel qualified.
I didn't feel ready.

But God had already chosen the day
my spirit would shift into assignment.

Activation didn't start with emotion,
excitement,
or spiritual fireworks.

It started with a **knowing.**

A quiet, unexplainable awareness
that something internal had turned
and I could never return
to who I was before.

Once Heaven activates you,
your life is no longer measured
by experiences
but by **assignments.**

And Heaven will not ask
for your permission
before it unlocks
your identity.

That was the day God activated me.

CHAPTER 2 — THE SILENT SWITCH

Activation does not begin with noise —
it begins with **inner interruption.**

Not the kind that disturbs your peace,
but the kind that alters your perception.

People think activation feels supernatural,
sensational,
or emotionally overwhelming.

Sometimes it does —
but sometimes it feels like
your internal compass
quietly turning
toward something you never planned.

My environment did not change —
my perception did.

What I once walked past,
I began noticing.

What I once ignored,
I began discerning.

What I once accepted as normal,
I began identifying
as spiritually informed.

This was not paranoia,
fear,
or insecurity.

It was Heaven pulling back the curtain
while everyone else
continued as if nothing shifted.

My silence was not confusion —
it was **new awareness.**

CHAPTER 3 — THE SURVEILLANCE OF THE SPIRIT

God did not activate me
to start talking more —
He activated me
to start **seeing more.**

People mistake quietness
for weakness.
But Heaven uses silence
as a classroom.

My silence became
my strongest weapon —
because while others
spoke freely,
I was receiving
spiritual data.

I was no longer seeing
faces, attitudes, and personalities —
I was seeing **operation, atmosphere, and intent.**

This was the moment
I learned that discernment
is not emotional sensitivity —
it is **spiritual intelligence.**

CHAPTER 4 — SPIRITUAL INTELLIGENCE TRAINING

God began training me
without announcing boot camp.

Lessons came without lectures.
Revelation came without explanation.
Understanding came without language.

I began discerning:

- Atmosphere shifts
- Hidden intention
- Unspoken hostility
- Silent alliances
- Invisible tension
- Spirit-to-spirit communication

Discernment was not to accuse —
but to **identify.**

This was not suspicion —
it was **instruction.**

Heaven was teaching me
to see what could not be spoken.

This was training —
not trauma.

CHAPTER 5 — DISCERNMENT DEPLOYMENT

Discernment is not an emotion —
it is a **tool of spiritual governance.**

God was showing me
not what people were doing
but what **was operating behind it.**

Not so I could react
but so I could **recognize.**

Discernment is not used
to expose, embarrass, confront, or punish.

It is used to
navigate, avoid, intercede, protect, and obey.

True discernment
does not need confirmation —
it needs **consecration.**

CHAPTER 6 — THE VAULT WITHIN

Authority is never granted externally —
it is **revealed internally.**

Inside every activated believer
is a vault that contains:

- Identity
- Wisdom
- Rank
- Immunity
- Revelation
- Codes
- Access
- Instructions

This vault is not discovered
through curiosity
but through **calling.**

Once the vault opens,
you stop trying
to be understood by people
who were never assigned
to interpret you.

CHAPTER 7 — EVIDENCE OF ACTIVATION

Evidence does not begin
in your mouth —
it begins in your **behavior.**

Activation produces:

- Silence over reaction
- Observation over confrontation
- Purpose over comfort
- Presence over performance
- Clarity over confusion
- Identity over insecurity
- Assignment over approval

Those who carry
real spiritual authority
do not strive
to be seen.

They understand that
identity is not proven —
it is **recognized.**

CHAPTER 8 — AUTHORITY RECOGNITION

Authority cannot be claimed —
only **recognized.**

When spiritual authority
is present,
reactions around you
change.

Some people withdraw,
some follow,
some observe,
some imitate,
some test,
some rebel,
some monitor.

None of these responses
define you —
they **reveal your impact.**

Real authority does not announce itself.
It carries
spiritual resonance.

CHAPTER 9 — THE LEGAL REALM OF IDENTITY

Identity is not emotional —
it is **legal.**

Hell does not respond
to your feelings —
it responds
to your **rank.**

Some battles are not attacks —
they are verification scans.

When Heaven activates identity,
Hell detects authority.

You are not fighting
to prove yourself —
you are resisting
so you **do not surrender
what Heaven already verified.**

CHAPTER 10 — THE QUIET GENERAL

A quiet general
is not trained
through applause
but through **obscurity.**

Hidden seasons are not delays —
they are **developmental sanctuaries.**

People assume that
the loudest, most visible personalities
carry the greatest authority.

But spiritual rank
is not based on
visibility
or popularity.

It is based on
**assignment compliance,
obedience,
and capacity.**

Quiet generals
shift atmospheres
without speaking
and influence outcomes
without position.

Once activated,
you begin receiving
instructional knowledge
without previous study.

This is not ego —
it is **download protocol.**

You begin noticing
timing, patterns, cues, and signals
that previously
meant nothing.

You are not being paranoid —
you are being **briefed.**

Documentation becomes
a spiritual discipline.

You are no longer
collecting moments —
you are collecting
intelligence.

CHAPTER 12 — WHEN ASSIGNMENT BECOMES IDENTITY

At first, activation feels
like something
that *happened to you.*

Eventually,
you realize it is
who you've always been.

You shift from seeking validation
to walking in confirmation.

Your prayers change from:
"Lord, take it away,"
to:
"Lord, train me in it."

Your confidence
is no longer in
your experience
but in **God's selection.**

When assignment becomes identity,
you stop running
from what you carry
and begin walking
in what Heaven authorized.

WHEN YOU DIDN'T KNOW YOU WERE SENT

Some people know they are called.
Others are activated before they ever understand what they're carrying.

Not everyone awakens with language.
Some awaken through movement.

You didn't know you were being sent.
You didn't know the ground mattered.
You didn't know the silence was training.

You thought you were surviving.
Heaven knew you were being positioned.

Activation does not always arrive with clarity.
Sometimes it arrives disguised as disruption, relocation, or pressure you cannot explain.

You didn't volunteer for spiritual conflict.
You were drawn into assignment before you had words for it.

Only later do you realize:

You were not lost.
You were deployed.

What felt like confusion was instruction.
What felt like resistance was calibration.
What felt like isolation was insulation.

You were not late to purpose.
You were early to awareness.

And now that you can see, you understand why environments shifted around you before you ever spoke.

You weren't trying to change anything.
You were changed — and everything else responded.

FOR THE ONE WHO DIDN'T KNOW

This book is not written for those who already identified themselves as anything spiritual.

It is written for the one who didn't know they were sent.

The one who thought they were enduring when they were actually being trained.
The one who felt pressure before they felt clarity.
The one who carried weight without explanation.

If this book found you after the fact, that is not coincidence.

Activation often explains itself **after obedience**.

Now that you know, you are not required to become louder.
You are only required to remain aligned.

EPILOGUE — THE QUIET CROWN

I was not activated
to be seen
or praised.

I was activated
to **recognize, interpret, and obey.**

What happened around me
does not define me.

What God awakened in me
established me.

Not defined
by the weapon that formed,
but authorized
by the God
who did not allow it
to prosper.

This is not the end —
it is the **commissioning.**

A quiet crown
does not glitter
to be noticed —
it stays steady
to be **trusted.**

So let it be.